Positions II:

# WHAT DO WE DO?

Written by Lindsay & Seth Little

Illustrated by Mark Harmon

LearnSport Books PUBLISHING CO

Meyer & Meyer Sport

British Library Cataloguing in Publication Data

A catalogue record for this book is available from the British Library

**What do we do?**



Aachen, Auckland, Beirut, Cairo, Cape Town, Dubai, Hägendorf, Hong Kong, Indianapolis, Manila, New Delhi, Singapore, Sydney, Tehran, Vienna

Member of the World Sport Publishers' Association (WSPA)

Manufacturing: Print Consult GmbH, Munich, Germany

ISBN 978-1-78255-099-0
E-Mail: info@m-m-sports.com, service@learnsportbooks.com
www.m-m-sports.com
www.learnsportbooks.com

iPlaySoccer

*May 2016*

# My Life in Soccer

*by Yael Averbuch*

Soft, green grass. Fun times with my family. Love and joy. Those are some of the first things that come to mind when I think about soccer.

I was seven years old when I watched my first soccer game. I didn't know anything about the sport besides that it seemed fun. My best friend in school invited me to come watch her game and my dad took me to cheer for her. That day, her team needed extra players and they asked me if I would play. I was very shy and said no. After watching her game, though, I decided that it looked like a lot of fun so my dad signed me up to play on a recreational team the next season.

I fell in love with the game at my first soccer practice, and have loved it ever since. It was a special time to share with my dad, as we learned about the game together. It was fun to be out on the field with my teammates and getting to play. And it was a whole new set of skills and experiences that made me very excited to learn.

When I was nine I wrote in my journal that I wanted to be a professional soccer player. I didn't really understand at the time what that meant, and

I certainly didn't know what it would take to get there. But I knew that I wanted to play for as long as I could and be the best I could be.

Since that time, soccer has taken me all across the world. I have played all over the U.S., in England, Germany, Holland, Japan, China, Australia, New Zealand, Thailand, Mexico, Canada, Sweden, Russia, Serbia and many other countries! I have also played for my country. I have formed friendships playing soccer that will last a lifetime. I have also learned a lot about myself through the game. I have learned what it takes to be a champion, and also how to overcome disappointments along the way.

Soccer is called "the beautiful game." There are so many reasons the sport is so beautiful and I'm sure that you will understand them as you play. I love soccer because there is such a variety of skills to learn. There are physical skills (like running fast, being strong, playing aggressively), skills with the ball (dribbling, trapping, shooting), and skills like teamwork and leadership. All are important to the game. There is no one right way to play soccer. It is a game of imagination and creativity.

I am now living the dream I have had since I was nine years old. I am a professional soccer player. It has not always been an easy path to accomplish my goals, but whenever I practice or play, I continue to love soccer more than ever.

Soon after I started playing, my dad and I began a mission to learn the game together. We would watch videos of soccer training and try to do the same drills in my backyard. I hope that you will enjoy learning and practicing the same way I did then, and have continued to do all my career.

I encourage you to learn and play the game of soccer, but most importantly, have fun while you do!

*Learn more about Yael Averbuch on her website: www.yaelaverbuch.com*
*Yael is also the founder of the Techne Futbol Training System, which helps players develop the skills necessary to play soccer and have fun: www.technefutbol.com*

I love game day! My team arrived at the field and started warming up.

“Alex!” my friend, Marco, called, “Are you sure you’re ready? We are playing the Dynamo. They are tough and crazy fast!”

Sam
Marco

The referees called our captains to the middle of the field.

We jogged onto the field and took our positions for kick off. Our parents cheered!

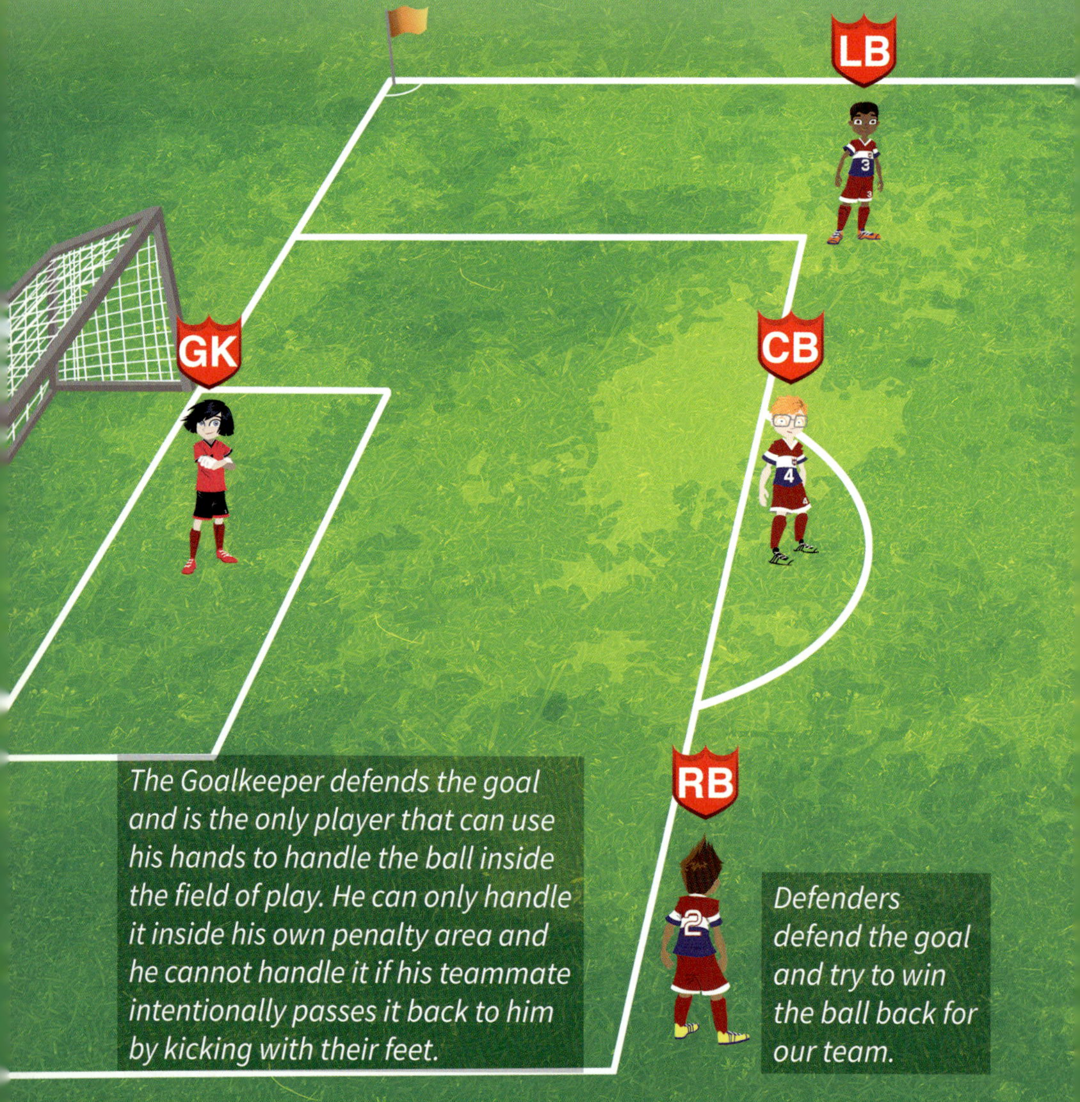


*The Goalkeeper defends the goal and is the only player that can use his hands to handle the ball inside the field of play. He can only handle it inside his own penalty area and he cannot handle it if his teammate intentionally passes it back to him by kicking with their feet.*

*Defenders defend the goal and try to win the ball back for our team.*

LM
Jaime, it's our kick. Come tap and play.
FW
RM
Midfielders take control of the ball, try to maintain possession of the ball by making smart passing decisions and create scoring opportunities. They play offense and defense, attacking and defending.
Forwards are responsible for creating scoring opportunities and taking shots on goal. They are also the first line of defense.

Madison yelled to us,
“Let’s go guys! Play fast!”

We kicked off, and both teams
started buzzing around the field.

*The other team plays defense. They will work together to protect their goal and attempt to take possession of the ball.*

*Alex's team is on offense. The forwards and midfielders will move towards the other team's goal trying to create scoring opportunities.*

Soon Madison gathered a heavy pass from Marco and was able to turn toward the Dynamo goal. She got her head up to look for teammates. I found an open space ahead of her and shouted, “Ball!”

She saw me and sent the ball flying my way. I trapped it softly with one of my best first touches ever and cut toward goal.

*Alex creates a scoring opportunity by identifying and moving towards empty space on the field. His teammate recognizes this and passes the ball.*

*Forwards, or Strikers, should always be paying attention and putting themselves in good positions, but they need to be careful to stay onside.*

Just then a Dynamo defender ran toward me. She was fast! I tried to cut around her and take a quick shot, but just as I fired another defender stepped in front and blocked my shot.

"It's OK, Alex, keep trying to find shots. Now go help defend!" Coach said.

The game never seemed to calm down. Thankfully, Sam was able to make some big saves to bail out the rest of us and keep us in the game.

After a few minutes, coach subbed me out.

“Thanks,” I said to Coach, gasping for air, “I can barely keep up. Their midfielders are everywhere!”

*Forwards are the first line of defense. It is important that forwards "press" and quickly pressure the opposing team's defenders that have the ball, especially right after they turn the ball over.*

*Although the forward may sometimes retreat into his team's half of the field to help defend, he should generally let his defenders win the ball and give them an outlet for passing.*

*Midfielders are extremely important in times of transition. The ball changes possession in the midfield more than on any other place on the field.*

*Midfielders need to regain possession of the ball every chance they get and maintain possession by making good decisions and smart passes.*

*An "attacking mid" is an offensive midfielder that plays closer to the other team's goal helping to create successful attacks.*

As usual, Madison led our team in winning the ball back into our possession and moving it quickly toward the Dynamo goal. She plays defense and offense, and she always transitions quickly.

We sure needed busy midfielders for this game; the Dynamo were flying around.

Coach subbed me back on to start the second half. Quickly, the Dynamo pushed the ball into our defensive half. Our defenders could barely hold off waves of attacks.

I stayed up field in my forward position ready to receive a pass and start a counter-attack once we won the ball back.

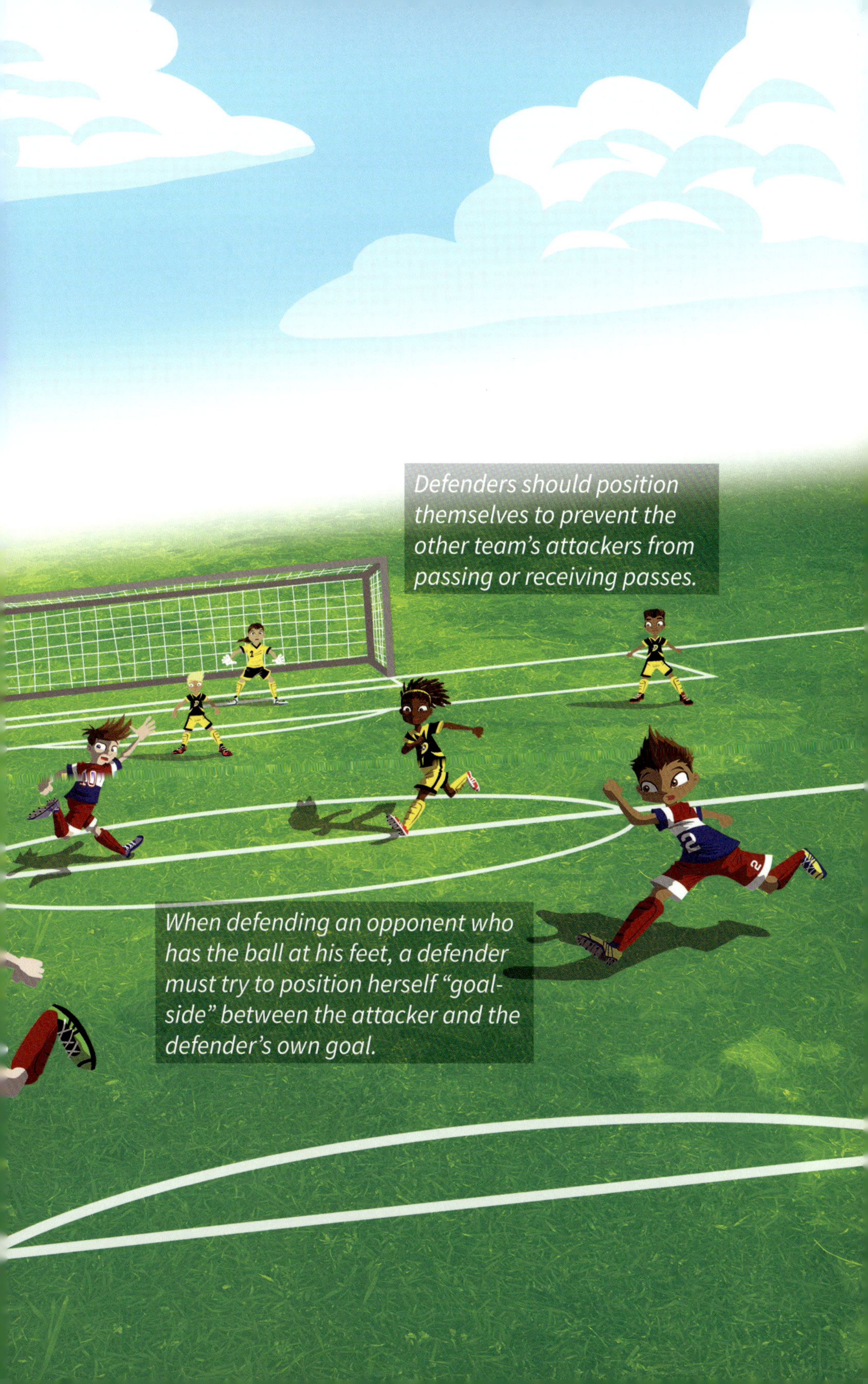

*Defenders should position themselves to prevent the other team's attackers from passing or receiving passes.*

*When defending an opponent who has the ball at his feet, a defender must try to position herself "goal-side" between the attacker and the defender's own goal.*

Suddenly, Marco stepped in and tackled the ball away from their forward. He passed it to Madison who had opened up between two Dynamo players in midfield.

Our whole team transitioned into attack mode.

*Defenders must talk to each other and listen to the goalkeeper in order to know who to mark and when to cover for a teammate.*

*Even though defenders mostly play in their own half of the field, they can create counter-attacks if they can win the ball and quickly advance it toward the other team's goal.*

“Alex!” Madison shouted. “Through ball, GO!” She slipped a pass through two defenders right into my path just after I started sprinting.

Luckily, I was careful to time my run so that I was onside when Madison kicked the ball forward to me.

*Goalkeepers will learn to cut off angles and guard their near post. After a save, the goalkeeper should get back on her feet as soon as possible.*

The Dynamo goalkeeper moved slightly closer to me and toward the goal post I was approaching. It really cut down my angle to shoot! Right before I went to take my set up touch to blast a shot, I heard Madison yell "Alex, back to me!" She had kept running and was now wide open.

I push passed the ball over to her with the inside of my foot and she fired it first time right in stride! It was a glorious shot, but incredibly, the keeper dove across the face of goal and saved it!

The ball deflected off the Dynamo keeper's hands and bounced straight back to me!

I was surprised, but I remembered what coach taught us about taking a volley shot. I focused on timing my kick just right so I could get my knee over the ball and lock my foot down as I came through it.

I caught it right on my laces, and it came off my foot like a rocket!

Goal! I love soccer!

"Soccer is a unique sport," Coach said, "because each of you needs to think for yourself and understand what your teammates are doing. As you gain experience and knowledge, you will develop a 'soccer brain' which will help you make good decisions on the field."

"The most important thing is that learning to play your position teaches you responsibility and accountability, which will help you your whole life."

# Teaching Concepts & Vocabulary

**Technique**: the ability to efficiently perform a task or specific soccer movement.

**Tactic**: an action performed by a player or group of players to take advantage of an opponent, group of opponents or a team. The tactics are the tools to develop the strategy.

**Strategy**: a general plan of action intended to win the game that is agreed upon by the team at the beginning of the game. The strategy relates to the formation and/or system used by the team.

**Formation**: the shape of the team and distribution of the players on the field at the beginning of the game. This is usually expressed in three numbers identifying the number of players in the defensive, midfield and attacking lines. Example: 4-3-3 indicates 4 defenders, 3 midfielders and 3 forwards.

**System**: a formation with additional specifications for the shape and/or the roles for one or more players. Systems combine formation and strategy. Example: 4-4-2 with diamond in midfield and outside backs moving up into wide areas.

**Keep shape**: to stay organized in positions on the field relative to the location of teammates and the ball.

**Transition**: The switch from playing offense to playing defense, or from defense to offense, which occurs when the ball changes possession. This is often the most important time in any soccer game.

**Counter-attack**: an immediate attack by one team that is triggered when an attack from the opposing team breaks down and the ball changes possession.

**Cover defense**: when a teammate is out of position or has been beaten, and the opposing attacking team exploits this area, the defender that is next closest to that area must recognize this and cover the area between his goal and where the attacker has broken through. The next closest player must recognize that event and move to defend the next most dangerous attacker until the attack is slowed and the team can regain its shape.

**Pack ball**: running with or toward a teammate without purpose and getting in the way of the teammate with the ball, like a puppy that wants to play. It is the failure to open up and create space.

**Ball-watching**: watching teammates play instead of becoming involved in the action in a positive manner by moving around and helping teammates.

**Showing for ball**: using movement to present for the ball between or in front of defenders. If the ball isn't passed immediately upon showing for it, the player should move to create a different passing option. Usually the best option is to retreat behind the next closest defender and then move laterally to present for the ball again.

# Approach

The iPlaySoccer books Positions 1 & 2 have been specifically designed to assist children in the transition from the 4v4 format of play to the 7v7 format, wherein positioning is formally introduced. The books have attempted to incorporate and apply the principles set forth in US Soccer's 2015 Player Development Initiatives, which were released to the general public in 2015 and requested to be implemented by the calendar year of 2017.

Among those initiatives are recommended positions and formations for both the 7v7 game play format and the 9v9 game play format. Instead of writing separate books for each, we elected to try and simplify these new concepts for children of this age classification by solely utilizing the commonly recommended 3-2-1 formation. We recognize there are many formation options that many very reputable and qualified youth coaches utilize, and by no means do we attempt to dictate what formation a coach elects to use, or attempt to discredit one formation as to another. Rather, these books represent an introduction to the format of play and to some of the concepts and vocabulary players will start to hear at they move along their soccer journey.

Among these new Player Development Initiatives are revised standards which provide for 4v4 play through age 7, and commencing with the U9 age classification the transition to 7v7 play with the introduction of positions, including a goal keeper, the use of formations, and the offside law.

# Team Organization

The Team Organization for the U9 and U10 includes a recommendation to utilize either a 2-3-1 formation designed to develop passing and movement of the ball or a 3-2-1 formation designed to promote forward runs and 1v1 situations. US Soccer provided indications as to suggested roles of the players in either position. This assignment of player numbers is remarkable as it represents a suggested style of play.

Traditionally, positions have been assigned a number to correspond with their primary function. The traditional numbering system makes the most sense when viewed within a 4-5-1 formation where the numbering system provides for 4 Defenders, 5 Midfielders, and 1 Forward. While there exist competing numbering systems that may assign different roles to different numbers, a traditional numbering system can be thought of as follows:

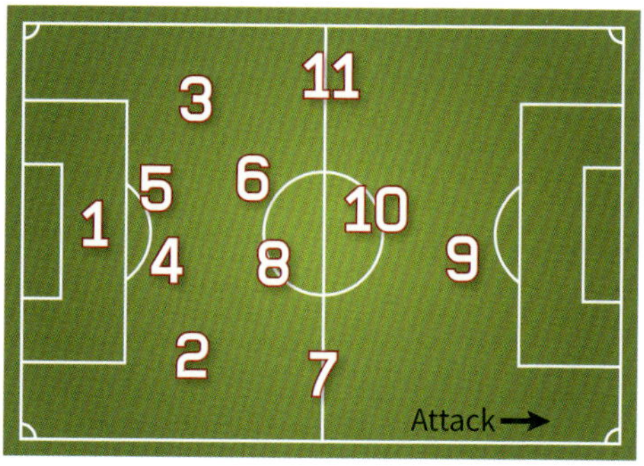


1 **Goalkeeper**: typically a good shot stopper with strong decision making ability and technically proficient in distribution.

2 **Outside Back**: defender with proficiency in 1v1 defending and physically capable to cover the flanks.

3 **Outside back**: plays opposite the Number 2.

4 **Center Back**: defender that is physically strong to win dispositive challenges on the ground and in the air, and must be mentally capable to help organize the defense.

5 **Center Back**: plays opposite the Number 4.

6 **Defensive Midfielder**: defense-oriented player able to cover ground, capable of winning challenges on the ground and in the air and willing to enter into tackles, win and keep possession.

7 **Outside Midfielder/Winger**: must be capable of covering the outside flank, possess a high work rate to make attacking runs but recover to defend, be able to take on defenders 1v1 and provide service into the box.

8 **Center Midfielder**: must be composed and calm on the ball, possess good vision and passing ability, capable of covering a large area of the field and proficient in organizing attacks and defense.